Hi! I'm Brian. Your brain is a very important part of your body and it does lots of important jobs. Let me tell you all about it…

Hi Brian! Great! I have lots of questions about what my brain does…

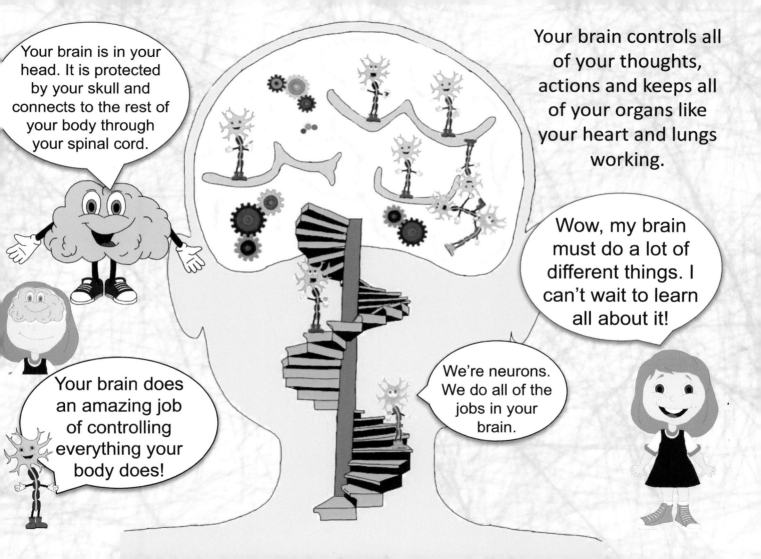

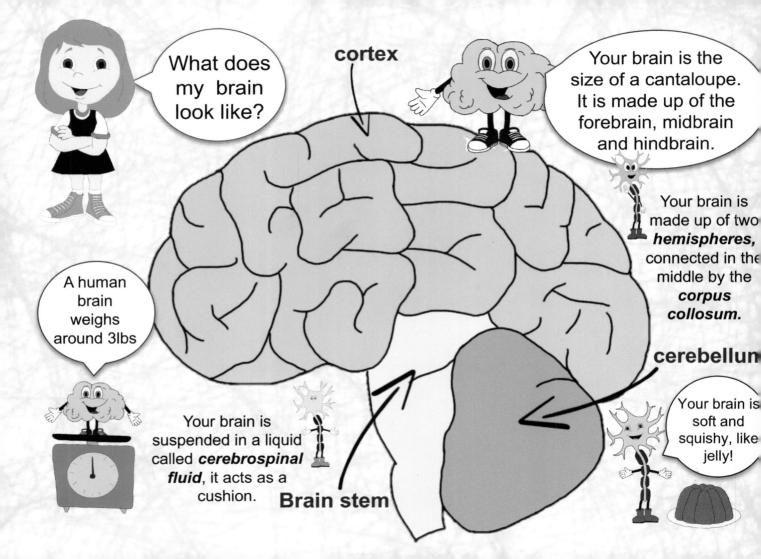

Let's take a picture of your brain. We can use an MRI scanner. An fMRI scan can show us how your brain looks and which parts are active. It shows changes in blood flow, areas you are using have a higher blood flow.

An MRI scanner is a very strong, giant magnet. The magnetic field is what allows us to see inside your brain.

fMRI stands for *functional magnetic resonsance*.

I'm excited to see what my brain looks like!

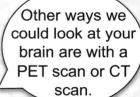

Other ways we could look at your brain are with a PET scan or CT scan.

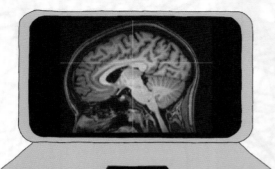

This is a view of your brain from the inside. The MRI scanner allows us to see the inside of your brain from outside your head!

All of the folds in your brain increase it's *surface area*.

That's really cool! I can see my own brain! Why is it so wrinkly Brian?

Well, your brain has to do lots of different jobs. It needs a lot of space to do this. If your brain was laid out flat without all of these folds, your head would need to be ginormous to fit it all in!

What is my brain made up of?

The human brain is made up of about 100 billion neurons and 1 trillion other cells.

Every neuron connects to lots of other neurons, every one can have up to 10 000 connections!

Cell body

Your brain is 75% water!

Each neuron has a different job to do. There are up to 10 000 different types of neuron in your brain.

dendrites

Us neurons are really small. You could fit 30 000 on the head of a pin.

myelin

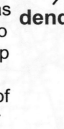

axon

You had more brain cells as a new born baby than you will ever have again!

What do neurons do?

Some neurons are over 1 metre long!

Neurons communicate with each other to send information to different parts of your brain and your body – so that you can move, see, talk, smell, taste, learn, remember and make decisions.

Information in your brain moves at 260 miles per hour – that's faster than a race car!

Your brain can produce enough energy to power a light bulb!

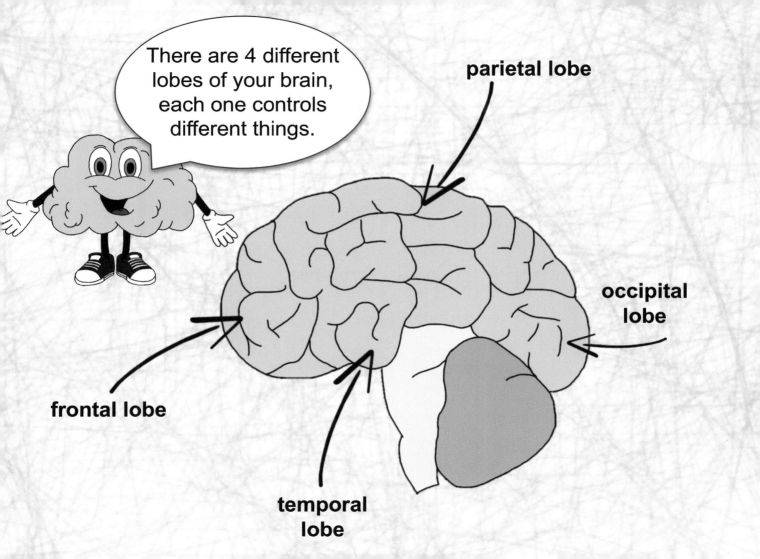

Parietal Lobe
Touch, pressure, temperature and pain

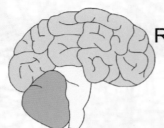

Frontal Lobe
Reasoning, planning, speech, movement, emotions and problem-solving

Occipital Lobe
Vision

Temporal Lobe
Hearing and memory

Your brain may be divided into lobes, but they all work together.

Even though your eyes are at the front of your head, in front of your brain, the part of your brain that controls how you see is in the back!

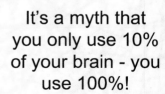

It's a myth that you only use 10% of your brain - you use 100%!

Brian, does my dog have a brain just like me?

Yes, all animals have a brain of some kind. Some animals have much bigger brains than others.

My brain is very similar to your human brain. This is why ape and monkey brains are really useful for scientists to study.

A cat's brain weighs 30g.

Laboratory mice give scientists a very good idea of how the human brain works.

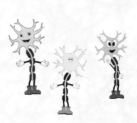

Humans have the largest brain in comparison to body size – your brain is 2% of your body weight.

The first brain '*connectome*' found by scientists was the brain of a worm called C. Elegans.

The brain of a fly only has 250 000 neurons.

Complex human brains like yours have **evolved** over millions and millions of years from the brains of much simpler animals, like worms.

Whales have the biggest brains, they weigh nearly 8kg!

The neurons in all animals work the same way. It is much easier for scientists to study how the brains or nervous systems of simpler invertebrates like worms work.

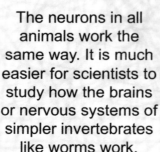

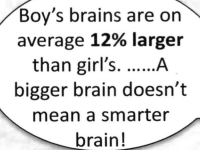

Do boys and girls have different brains?

Girls often have a larger **hippocampus** than boys. This is the part of the brain in control of memory – maybe this means girls are better at remembering!

Brain researchers have found differences between men and women in the size of the connection between the two **hemispheres** of the brain – the **corpus collosum**.

Boy's brains are on average **12% larger** than girl's. ......A bigger brain doesn't mean a smarter brain!

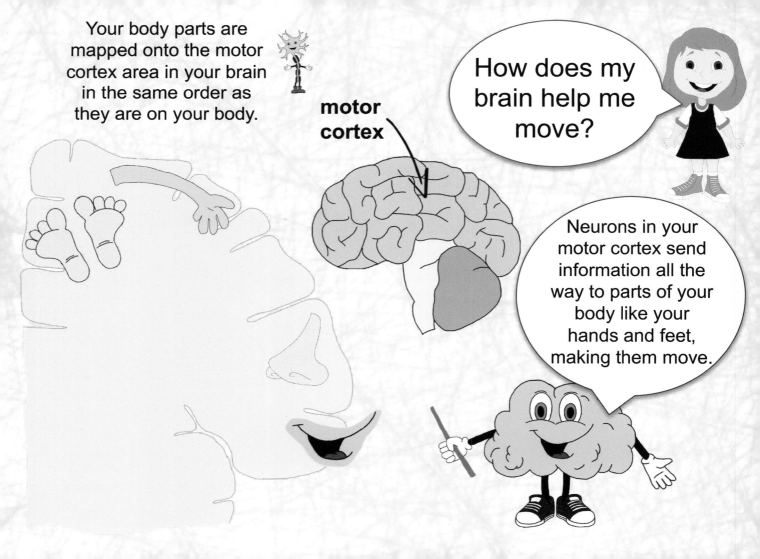

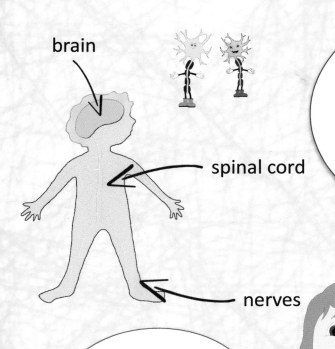

brain

spinal cord

nerves

Your brain is connected to every part of your body through nerves. Some of these nerves are motor neurons – this means they help you move parts of your body.

Wow! My brain can send information really far away!

The left side of your body is controlled by the right side of your brain, and the right side of your body is controlled by the left side of your brain.

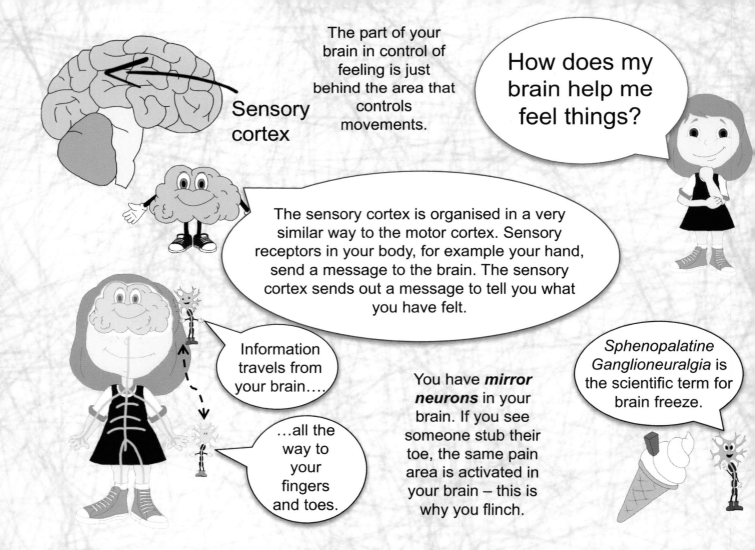

If your body parts were proportional to the amount of space in your brain that controls them, then you would look pretty strange!

Your brain has no pain receptors, so you cannot feel pain in your brain.

You can't tickle yourself because your brain can predict what is going to happen.

The torso, legs and feet of the homunculus are small because there are fewer touch receptors here.

There are lots of touch receptors in your mouth and tongue.

This is an *homunculus*. This is how you would look if your body was proportional to it's representation in the sensory area of your brain.

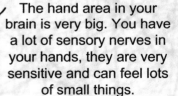

The hand area in your brain is very big. You have a lot of sensory nerves in your hands, they are very sensitive and can feel lots of small things.

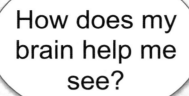

How does my brain help me see?

There are special cells inside your eyes called *photoreceptors*. They send information from the world you see to your brain.

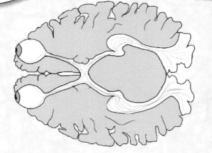

Everything you see on your left goes to the right side of your brain, things you see on your right go to the left side.

cone

I help you see the difference between light and dark.

I help you see the difference between colours.

rod

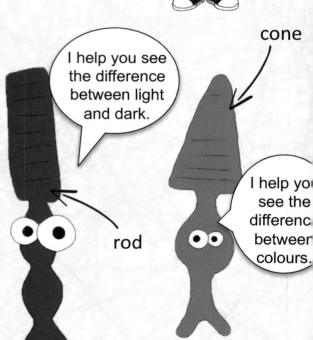

You cannot see colours well at night because cones don't work well in dim light.

How does my brain help me remember things?

Your brain has two types of memory store. 1. Short term memory. 2. Long term memory.

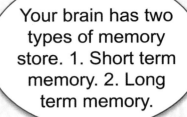

Short term memory holds a small amount of information for a short period of time.

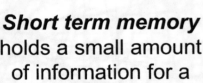

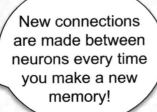

New connections are made between neurons every time you make a new memory!

Long term memory allows you to store information for a very long time and access it a long time in the future.

Forgetting is good for your brain. Removing information you don't need helps your brain to keep building new connections.

How does my brain help me learn new things?

Every time you experience something new, a new connection is made between neurons in your brain. The more you do something, the stronger the new connection becomes.

The ability of your brain to make and change connections between neurons is called *neural plasticity.*

When you learn something new, the structure of your brain changes!

The brain's storage capacity is virtually unlimited, it doesn't get used up like storage on a computer.

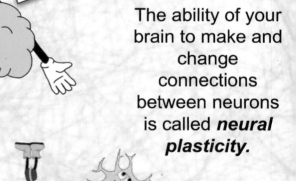

Does my brain control if I am happy or angry?

Different emotions are controlled by different areas of your brain.

Laughing is controlled by 5 different brain areas!

Anger is controlled by a part of your brain called the *amygdala*. The amygdala sends information to another area which gets you ready to either run away or fight the thing that has made you angry. This is called the *fight or flight response*.

Emotions are linked to your memories. Remembering how you felt when something happened can be triggered by something you heard, saw or even smelt.

Your brain has pleasure centres, where feel good chemicals are released. These are triggered by things that make you feel happy.

How does my brain help me taste?

There are 5 basic tastes – *sweet, salty, sour, bitter & umami*. You have taste buds on your tongue, which are made up of lots of different taste receptors. Taste receptors send information from your mouth to your brain.

bitter

sour   sour

umami

salty   salty

sweet

Chocolate contains a chemical called *phenylethylamine* – also known as the love drug because it makes your pulse faster, as though you are in love.

You don't only have taste receptors in your mouth, they are also in your stomach, intestines, lungs and brain!

Taste receptors live for only 1 or 2 weeks and then are replaced by new receptors.

How does my brain help me hear?

Sound waves cause your eardrum and tiny bones inside your ear to vibrate. This generates a *nerve impulse.* Nerves carry information of the nerve impulse from your ears to your brain. Your brain can then decipher the sound.

Dogs and other mammals can hear higher pitched sounds than humans.

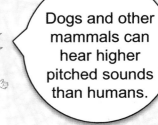

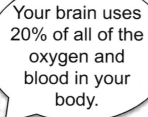

What does my brain do when I'm asleep?

When you are resting, your brain is still active. It is using around 1/5 calorie every minute. Some brain waves are actually more active when you are asleep than when you are awake.

12% of people dream in black & white

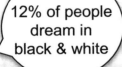

Yawning provides your brain with extra oxygen and cools in down

Everyone dreams, you have between 4 and 7 dreams every night. Scientists think that dreams are symbolic representations of things in your real life made by your *unconscious*.

Your brain goes through a sleep cycle every night. 20% of this cycle is *REM sleep* – this is when you dream.

What happens when something goes wrong in the brain?

Some children have a difficulty with reading and writing caused by a difference in their brain, called *dyslexia*. Scientists think that the language area of the brains of dyslexic children works differently to the brains of other children.

If part of the brain is injured, it can effect things you do that the area controls. For example, people who have a **stroke** often have trouble with speaking because the speech area of their brain has been damaged.

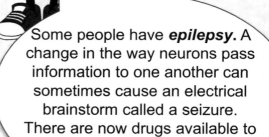

Some people have *epilepsy.* A change in the way neurons pass information to one another can sometimes cause an electrical brainstorm called a seizure. There are now drugs available to control epilepsy and stop seizures from happening.

Sometimes, if one part of the brain is damaged then another part can learn to do it's job.

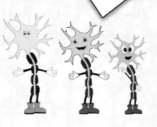

What do brain scientists do?

Lots of different scientists research how the brain works.

Neuroscientists study the biology of the brain and nervous system.

Some neuroscientists investigate how brain cells are organised and how all of the neurons in your brain are connected.

Neuroscience research is very exciting and important in improving our understanding of how our brains work.

Other neuroscientists investigate *chemical reactions* in the brain and their relationship with different actions and behaviours.

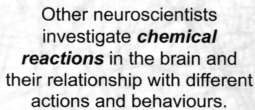

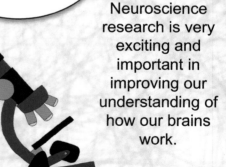

Researchers in *psychology* study the brain in a different way. *Neuropsychologists* are interested in how your brain is involved in different behaviours and actions.

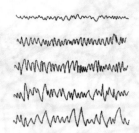

Some neuropsychologists study brain activity by measuring brain waves with **EEG**.

Some psychologists look at brain activity using *neuroimaging*, like the **MRI** scanner. Brain imaging lets them see which areas of the brain are active while you do certain things.

There are lots of different ways that different scientists study the brain and how it works. All of the different types of research mean they can find out as much about the brain as possible.